For

EVERLASTING

Friendship

A Bouquet of Loving
Thoughts

Edited by Evelyn L. Beilenson

Design by Lesley Ehlers
Photographs by Solomon M. Skolnick

PETER PAUPER PRESS, INC.
WHITE PLAINS, NEW YORK

Pressed flower art by Tauna Andersen
courtesy of *Pressed for Time*, Ephraim, Utah

Copyright © 1995
Peter Pauper Press, Inc.
202 Mamaroneck Avenue
White Plains, NY 10601
ISBN 0-88088-882-2
Printed in Singapore
7 6 5 4 3 2 1

Contents

Everlasting Friendship

A friend may well be reckoned the master-piece of nature.

Ralph Waldo Emerson

Introduction

*E*verlastings, or dried flowers, retain the essence of their shape and color long after they have been picked. Similarly, friendships, lovingly tended, last long after the first introduction, maintaining their important place in our lives.

If we are fortunate, we have many friends with whom we exchange gifts, whether a simple smile, love, admiration, or consolation.

For centuries, people have availed themselves of dried flowers to express their feelings or emotions in a language of flowers. Everlastings are voices of nature and express friendship and love through a myriad of our senses—touch, smell, and sight.

In this Keepsake, we are using key words from the language of flowers to celebrate the many aspects of friendship. May these flowers and your friendships last forever!

E. L. B.

African Daisy

SIMPLICITY, INNOCENCE

The most I can do for my friend is simply to be his friend.

Henry David Thoreau

I adore simple pleasures. They are the last refuge of the complex.

Oscar Wilde

Simplicity of character is no hindrance to subtlety of intellect.

John Morley

The simple joy of having a friend is exceeded only by the simple joy of being a friend.

Sarah Carr

Amaranthus

IMMORTALITY

We never know the true value of friends. While they live we are too sensitive of their faults: when we have lost them we only see their virtues.

J. C. and A. W. Hare

People come and go in life, but they never leave your dreams. Once they're in your subconscious, they are immortal.

Patricia Hampl

The people I respect most behave as if they were immortal and as if society was eternal.

E. M. Forster

Perhaps nature is our best assurance of immortality.

Eleanor Roosevelt

Ambrosia

LOVE RETURNED

So long as we are loved by others I should say that we are almost indispensable; and no man is useless while he has a friend.

Robert Louis Stevenson

Love means giving one's self to another person fully, not just physically. When two people really love each other, this helps them to stay alive and grow. One must really be loved to grow.

Nancy Reagan

If there is anything better than to be loved it is loving.

Anonymous

$\mathcal{Y}$ou don't have a garden just for yourself. You have it to share.

Augusta Carter

$\mathcal{Y}$ou are as welcome as the flowers in May.

Charles Macklin

$\mathcal{T}$here is no power on earth that can withstand the power of love. By loving our enemies we turn them into friends.

Stella Terrill Mann

$\mathcal{F}$riendship is a strong and habitual inclination in two persons to promote the good and happiness of one another.

Eustace Budgell

$\mathcal{L}$ove is, above all, the gift of oneself.

Jean Anouilh

Baby's Breath

GENTLENESS, EVERLASTING LOVE

The holy passion of Friendship is of so sweet and
steady and loyal and enduring a nature that it will
last through a whole lifetime, if not asked to lend
money.

Mark Twain

A true friend is forever a friend.

George Macdonald

*S*ome friendships grow and ripen steadily with the years. They have become part of our lives and we just accept them with sweet content and glad confidence. We have discovered that somehow we are rested and inspired by a certain comradeship; that we understand and are understood.

Hugh Black

*M*y coat and I live comfortably together. It has assumed all my wrinkles, does not hurt me anywhere, has moulded itself on my deformities, and is complacent to all my movements, and I only feel its presence because it keeps me warm. Old coats and old friends are the same thing.

Victor Hugo

Bachelor's Button

DELICACY, HOPE IN LOVE

Love has nothing to do with what you are expecting to get—only with what you are expecting to give—which is everything.

Katharine Hepburn

Love does not consist in gazing at each other but in looking outward together in the same direction.

Antoine de Saint-Exupéry

You must have love in your heart before you can have hope.

Yoruba proverb

Chrysanthemum

CHEERFULNESS

*T*hose who bring sunshine to the lives of others cannot keep it from themselves.

Sir James M. Barrie

*T*o you, my cheerful friend!—To you! who seem to be an exquisite architect, forever building up the castle of happiness out of all the losses and crosses and wrecks and ruins that fate may throw about you:—to you who can always see the silver lining to every cloud, who can conceal your sorrows and share your joys and laugh and sing, and be content, and still keep up the fight till life's rugged journey ends. To you, my friend!

Joseph D. Houston

Clematis Virginiana

MENTAL BEAUTY

Friendship is almost always the union of a part of one mind with a part of another; people are friends in spots.

George Santayana

A friend is a person with whom I may be sincere. Before him, I may think aloud.

Ralph Waldo Emerson

Even where the affections are not strongly moved by any superior excellence, the companions of our childhood always possess a certain power over our minds which hardly any later friend can obtain.

Mary Shelley

*E*ach person grows not only by her own talents and development of her inner beliefs, but also by what she receives from the persons around her.

Iris Haberli

*T*o be capable of steady friendship or lasting love are the two greatest proofs, not only of goodness of heart but of strength of mind.

William Hazlitt

*P*ure friendship is something which men of an inferior intellect can never taste.

Jean de La Bruyère

*E*veryone alters and is altered by everyone else. We are all the time taking in portions of one another or else reacting against them, and by these involuntary acquisitions and repulsions modifying our natures.

Gerald Brenan

Clover

Be Mine

*T*he entire sum of existence is the magic of being needed by just one person.

Vi Putnam

*T*he love we give away is the only love we keep.

Elbert Hubbard

*M*y heart shall be thy garden.

Alice Meynell

*W*on't you come into the garden? I would like my roses to see you.

Richard Brinsley Sheridan

Cross of Jerusalem

DEVOTION

My true friends have always given me that supreme proof of devotion, a spontaneous aversion for the man I loved.

Colette

No one perfectly loves God who does not perfectly love some of his creatures.

Marguerite de Valois

I never knew how to worship until I knew how to love.

Henry Ward Beecher

Delphinium

HEAVEN

I don't like to commit myself about heaven and
hell—you see, I have friends in both places.

Mark Twain

If a man could mount to Heaven and survey the
mighty universe, his admiration of its beauties
would be much diminished unless he had someone
to share in his pleasure.

Cicero

*H*eaven will be inherited by every man who has
heaven in his soul.

Henry Ward Beecher

Goldenrod

ENCOURAGEMENT

*T*here is no friend like an old friend
  Who has shared our morning days,
No greeting like his welcome,
  No homage like his praise.

Oliver Wendell Holmes

*T*here is no such thing as a "self-made" man. We are made up of thousands of others. Everyone who has ever done a kind deed for us, or spoken one word of encouragement to us, has entered into the make-up of our character and of our thoughts, as well as our success.

George Matthew Adams

*P*raise is the best diet for us, after all.

Sydney Smith

*M*y best friend is the man who in wishing me well
wishes it for my sake.

Aristotle

Heather

*O*nly solitary men know the full joys of friendship. Others have their family; but to a solitary and an exile his friends are everything.

Willa Cather

*F*riendship needs no words—it is solitude delivered from the anguish of loneliness.

Dag Hammarskjöld

*D*o not rely completely on any other human being, however dear. We meet all life's greatest tests alone.

Agnes Macphail

I never found the companion that was so companionable as solitude.

Henry David Thoreau

*I*nside myself is a place where I live all alone, and that's where you renew your springs that never dry up.

Pearl S. Buck

*S*olitude is the voice of Nature that speaks to us.

George Sand

*A*rranging a bowl of flowers in the morning can give a sense of quiet in a crowded day—like writing a poem, or saying a prayer.

Anne Morrow Lindbergh

Hydrangea

HEARTLESSNESS

Man's inhumanity to man
Makes countless thousands mourn!

Robert Burns

If we can still love those who made us suffer, we
can love them all the more.

Anna Jameson

It goes without saying that your friends are usual-
ly the first to discuss your personal business behind
your back.

Terry McMillan

All cruelty springs from hard-heartedness and weakness.

Seneca

No person is your friend who demands your silence or denies your right to grow.

Alice Walker

It is easier to forgive an enemy than to forgive a friend.

William Blake

If one of my friends happens to die, I drive down to St. James's Coffee House, and bring home a new one.

Horace Walpole

I've noticed your hostility towards him . . . I ought to have guessed you were friends.

Malcolm Bradbury

Iris

My Compliments

Sweet is the scene where genial friendship plays
The pleasing game of interchanging praise.

Oliver Wendell Holmes

Get someone else to blow your horn and the sound
will carry twice as far.

Will Rogers

I can live for two months on a good compliment.

Mark Twain

To cease to admire is a proof of deterioration.

Charles Horton Cooley

Larkspur

LEVITY

If you cannot lift the load off another's back, do not walk away. Try to lighten it.

Frank Tyger

We cherish our friends not for their ability to amuse us, but for ours to amuse them.

Evelyn Waugh

That is the best—to laugh with someone because you both think the same things are funny.

Gloria Vanderbilt

A light heart lives long.

William Shakespeare

$\mathscr{W}$it . . . is, after all, a form of arousal. We challenge one another to be funnier and smarter. It's high-energy play. It's the way friends make love to one another.

Anne Gottlieb

$\mathscr{A}$mong those whom I like, I can find no common denominator, but among those whom I love, I can: all of them make me laugh.

W. H. Auden

$\mathscr{T}$hose who do not know how to weep with their whole heart don't know how to laugh either.

Golda Meir

Lavender

It is more shameful to distrust our friends than to be deceived by them.

François de La Rochefoucauld

Love all, trust a few,
Do wrong to none; be able for thine
   enemy
Rather in power than use; and keep thy
   friend
Under thy own life's key.

William Shakespeare

I don't trust him. We're friends.

Bertolt Brecht

While your friend holds you affectionately by both your hands you are safe, for you can watch both his.

Ambrose Bierce

The more I traveled the more I realized that fear makes strangers of people who should be friends.

Shirley MacLaine

Even in the common affairs of life, in love, friendship, and marriage, how little security have we when we trust our happiness in the hands of others!

William Hazlitt

However much we may distrust men's sincerity, we always believe they speak to us more sincerely than to others.

François de La Rochefoucauld

Marigold

I hold it true, whate'er befall;
I feel it, when I sorrow most;
'Tis better to have loved and lost
Than never to have loved at all.

Alfred, Lord Tennyson

*W*hoever has loved knows all that life contains of
sorrow and of joy.
The breaking of a heart leaves no traces.

George Sand

I can't forgive my friends for dying; I don't find
these vanishing acts of theirs at all amusing.

Logan Pearsall Smith

$\mathcal{T}$rue friendship is like sound health; the value of it is seldom known until it is lost.

Charles Caleb Colton

$\mathcal{S}$orrow is a fruit; God does not allow it to grow on a branch that is too weak to bear it.

Victor Hugo

$\mathcal{W}$hen I hear that a friend has fallen into matrimony, I feel the same sorrow as if I had heard of his lapsing into theism.

Algernon Swinburne

$\mathcal{W}$hen a friend dies, part of yourself dies too.

St. John Irvine

$\mathcal{T}$hose who have suffered understand suffering and therefore extend their hand.

Patti Smith

Myrtle

LOVE

Greater love hath no man than this, that a man lay down his life for his friends.

John 15:13 (KJV)

Friendship is Love, without his wings!

Lord Byron

If we spend our lives in loving, we have no leisure to complain or to feel unhappiness.

Joseph Joubert

The more we love, the better we are; and the greater our friendships are, the dearer we are to God.

Jeremy Taylor

If we would build on a sure foundation in friendship, we must love friends for their sake rather than for our own.

Charlotte Brontë

Flowers are Love's truest language.

Park Benjamin

Love works miracles every day: such as weakening the strong, and strengthening the weak; making fools of the wise, and wise men of fools; favoring the passions, destroying reason, and, in a word, turning everything topsy-turvy.

Marguerite de Valois

Oriental Poppy

CONSOLATION

The timid hand stretched forth to aid
  A brother in his need;
A kindly word in grief's dark hour
  That proves a friend indeed . . .

Charles Dickens

He that is thy friend indeed,
He will help thee in thy need:
If thou sorrow, he will weep;
If thou wake, he cannot sleep;
Thus of every grief in heart,
He with thee doth bear a part.
These are certain signs to show
Faithful friend from faltering foe.

Richard Barnfield

Peony

BASHFULNESS

*U*nder the magnetism of friendship the modest man becomes bold; the shy, confident; the lazy, active; or the impetuous, prudent and peaceful.

William Makepeace Thackeray

*D*o not be too timid and squeamish about your actions. All life is an experiment.

Ralph Waldo Emerson

*T*hough modesty be a virtue, yet bashfulness is a vice.

Thomas Fuller

*T*he most frightening part of helping is getting involved.

Dianne Ridley Roberts

Rose

BEAUTY

For every beauty there is an eye somewhere
    to see it.
For every truth there is an ear somewhere
    to hear it.
For every love there is a heart somewhere
    to receive it.

Ivan Panin

He who cannot see the beautiful side is a bad
painter, a bad friend, a bad lover; he cannot lift his
mind and his heart so high as goodness.

Joseph Joubert

Happiness itself is sufficient excuse. Beautiful
things are right and true; so beautiful actions are
those pleasing to the gods.

Aristotle

Sage

ESTEEM

*T*he happiest moments it [my heart] knows are those in which it is pouring forth its affections to a few esteemed characters.

Thomas Jefferson

*O*ften intimacies between women go backwards, beginning with revelations and ending up in small talk without loss of esteem.

Elizabeth Bowen

*L*ove is an expression and assertion of self-esteem, a response to one's own values in the person of another.

Ayn Rand

*H*e removes the greatest ornament of friendship
who takes away from it respect.

Cicero

*T*he friendships which last are those wherein each
friend respects the other's dignity to the point of
not really wanting anything from him.

Cyril Connolly

*S*o much is a man worth as he esteems himself.

Rabelais

*F*riendship, compounded of esteem and love,
derives from one its tenderness and its permanence
from the other.

Samuel Johnson

Sorrel

JOY

*T*rue friends have no solitary joy or sorrow.
William Ellery Channing

*W*ho knows the joys of friendship?
The trust, security, and mutual tenderness,
The double joys where each is glad for both?
Nicholas Rowe

*J*oys divided are increased.

Josiah Gilbert Holland

*T*o want friendship is a great fault. Friendship
ought to be a gratuitous joy, like the joys afforded
by art, or life.

Simone Weil

Fellowship in joy, and not sympathy in sorrow,
makes people friends.

Friedrich Wilhelm Nietzsche

All human joys are swift of wing,
For heaven doth so allot it;
That when you get an easy thing,
You find you haven't got it.

Eugene Field

Love for the joy of loving, and not for the offer-
ings of someone else's heart.

Marlene Dietrich

❧ 49 ❧

Sweet William

A Smile

What sunshine is to flowers, smiles are to friend-ship.

Nicole Beale

Wear a smile and have friends; wear a scowl and have wrinkles. What do we live for if not to make the world less difficult for each other?

George Eliot

Let us make one point . . . that we meet each other with a smile, when it is difficult to smile. . . . Smile at each other, make time for each other in your family.

Mother Teresa

Thistle

AUSTERITY, MISANTHROPY

*L*ife is not worth living for the man who has not even one good friend.

Democritus of Abdera

*D*ie when I may, I want it said of me by those who know me best, that I always plucked a thistle and planted a flower where I thought a flower would grow.

Abraham Lincoln

*C*hoose a good disagreeable friend, if you are wise—a surly, steady, economical, rigid fellow.

William Makepeace Thackeray

He who throws away a friend is as bad as he who throws away his life.

Sophocles

The misanthropist is to be pitied when his despair proceeds from an ardent love for the good, the beautiful, and the true.

George Sand

I consider him an unhappy man whom no one pleases.

Martial

We walk alone in the world. Friends, such as we desire, are dreams and fables.

Ralph Waldo Emerson

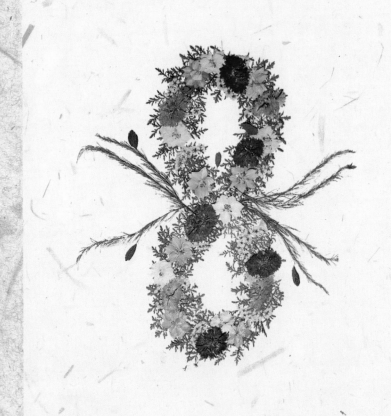

Tulip

DECLARATION OF LOVE

We discovered in each other and ourselves worlds, galaxies, a universe.

Anne Rivers Siddons

If thou lovest, thou wilt be loved.

Saint Francis

For what is love itself, for the one we love best?— an enfolding of immeasurable cares which yet are better than any joys outside our love.

George Eliot

A relationship is placing one's heart and soul in the hands of another while taking charge of another in one's soul and heart.

Kahlil Gibran

Familiar acts are beautiful through love.

Percy Bysshe Shelley

Never cease loving a person, and never give up hope for him, for even the prodigal son who had fallen most low could still be saved; the bitterest enemy and also he who was your friend could again be your friend; love that has grown cold can kindle again.

Søren Kierkegaard

All, everything that I understand, I understand only because I love.

Leo Tolstoy

Love is . . . born with the pleasure of looking at each other, it is fed with the necessity of seeing each other, it is concluded with the impossibility of separation!

José Martí

Yellow Yarrow

CURE FOR HEARTACHE

I was angry with my friend:
I told my wrath, my wrath did end.
I was angry with my foe:
I told it not, my wrath did grow.

William Blake

I do not want people to be very agreeable, as it
saves me the trouble of liking them a great deal.

Jane Austen

*E*ver since I could remember anything, flowers
have been like dear friends to me, comforters,
inspirers, powers to uplift and to cheer.

Celia Thaxter